A Carer's Chaos

Julie Nancy Wiltshire

Matador
9 Priory Business Park,
Wistow Road, Kibworth Beauchamp,
Leicestershire. LE8 0RX
Tel: 0116 279 2299
Email: books@troubador.co.uk
Web: www.troubador.co.uk/matador
Twitter: @matadorbooks

ISBN 978 1788035 958

British Library Cataloguing in Publication Data.
A catalogue record for this book is available from the British Library.

Printed by TJ International Ltd, Padstow, Cornwall, UK
Typeset in 11.5pt Cambria by Troubador Publishing Ltd, Leicester, UK

Matador is an imprint of Troubador Publishing Ltd

INTRODUCTION

This is a true story concerning my husband's insidious cancer (multiple plasmacytoma) which has occurred twice, and my experiences and traumas being the carer over a period of three years. This is a different slant on stories of cancer as it is told by the carer. We carers say that when a person with cancer has a partner it is not 'I have cancer,' it is 'WE have cancer.'

A CARER'S CHAOS

My life always seemed to be assembled like a big, beautiful complete jigsaw puzzle. The picture was colourful and bright, but suddenly, without warning, it was to be smashed by the cruel, twisted wrecking ball of cancer, leaving me broken in to pieces on the floor. My life would have to be rebuilt piece by piece. I only hoped the central piece of the jigsaw, my husband, would not become the missing piece. My husband's cancer changed my life. The things I once put value on did not matter. Material things were insignificant. Relationships with family and friends were most important and very precious. It tested my values. I had to change as a person, not to be afraid to ask for help, not to have such high expectations of people, and to learn the complexities of the human race. I had to learn how to release my anger quietly without hurting others. Hopefully, I have come out of it a different person as a result of my experiences and now possess the precious gift of humility, and also compassion for others struggling with health problems.

*

It all began on a shivery evening in December. The day had begun to cry its heavy tears of grief at the dying of the light. Hubby decided to go into his garage and rummage around in the roof space for the dreaded Christmas trimmings, greatly annoyed by my whining. Minutes later he burst through the kitchen door with all the trimmings spilling from his arms. He called across the kitchen, 'I think I'm on the way out.'

'What?' I replied, irritatedly. 'Why?'

'I know we are both stressed coming up to Christmas, but when I switched off the light in the garage I could see bright stars dancing all over the place.'

'Rubbish,' I snapped. 'You are imagining it.'

'You don't care,' he snapped back.

'Anyway,' I replied, tossing in a smattering of disinterest. 'If you are worried, I would go to the doctors''

He stood motionless, moulded into the moment.

*

The following day he begrudgingly made an appointment and trotted off to the doctors', luckily, receiving an appointment the same day. He hated doctors so I knew instantly he was quite concerned. He later came back to say he'd had blood tests taken and would soon know the results. Only a few days passed before the doctor telephoned, which seemed too quick for comfort, and said it would be best to cover all avenues and that he should see a blood specialist at the Gloucestershire Royal Hospital.

The letter from the hospital duly arrived. That was when we began the long hellish journey to where we are now. Fate held us in the palm of its hand.

We attended the appointment and were told the blood samples were normal, but the blood specialist was concerned about the flashing lights David had seen and felt maybe there were more tests to be done. He enquired whether there were any inherent health problems from my husband's family. My husband replied a little too speedily for comfort that there weren't any. I didn't want to seem a pushy wife, but I felt I had to intervene. 'Please can I speak,' I said hesitantly. The specialist arched his brow and peered over his glasses. 'It might be insignificant but my husband's father died from liver failure in his seventies and his sister also died from liver failure. The doctors thought both of them were drinkers, but that was not the case.' My husband gave me a sideways glance through his accelerated frown and rolled the whites of his eyes. The specialist paused for a moment and raised his hand in the air and clicked his fingers. 'Ah,' he replied, 'There is one blood test I think we should do to eliminate everything.' A nurse took David's blood again and we went home from (as we came to call it) Dracula's Ward. A few days passed and then a letter arrived to summon us once again to the Edward Jenner Ward at the Gloucestershire Royal Hospital for more blood tests and to see the specialist. We both began to feel a little uneasy. A light headache had crawled into my brain and had busied itself behind my weary eyes.

*

The following week, sat in Dr Freeman's room, we were told that David had hemochromatosis, a condition whereby the blood stores too much iron which can accumulate around the vital organs such as the liver, kidneys, and heart and be very dangerous, as the iron can cause irreversible damage. Dr Freeman asked David to get onto the couch whereby he proceeded to prod around the area of his liver. 'Um,' said Dr Freeman. 'Your liver seems fine in size, but your iron count is near 1000; comfortably, your reading should be 200-250. You need to attend the hospital every week for us to draw a pint of blood from you to bring the iron count down.' Our silence bounced around the room and swallowed up the air. That is what we did for weeks until the iron count dropped down to the required level. Our children and David's cousins had to be tested for the condition, but thankfully their results came back clear, although my daughter is a carrier. We were told David could eat nothing with too much iron in it like certain types of cereals fortified with iron or too much red meat such as liver or steak or too much fruit. Buying items in the supermarket became a quest to find the correct food. I read every label with a sudden urgency and had to always remember to take my reading glasses with me. I quarrelled incessantly with myself down the

4

aisles on what I should buy. My husband and I were told by a doctor that years ago they would give the bag of blood back to the hemochromatosis patients they had drawn it from to pour onto their flowers in their gardens (such as roses). Apparently, it is nutritional for plants. No such luck now, what with all the health and safety rules, so there are no more folk walking around with bags of blood from the Dracula Ward. I visualised all they would have needed in the past, besides the bags, would have been black flowing cloaks and sharp fangs. The imagery brought a wry smile to my face which was not acceptable in the face of adversity. Through the course of treatment they decided to give David a lumbar puncture to do some tests on his bone marrow. He was now on a closely watched regime and well and truly buried deep within the system.

*

I sat alongside David a few days later as he lay on the bed sideways with his knees up to his chest in the foetal position. He took on a look of vulnerability, which was so unfamiliar for such a big man. Like a dark bough snapped from a tree he rested on a sheet of snow ready to be broken again. The needle going into his back resembled the painful sting of an intolerant bee; I had to glance away. Shortly the tests came back and we were told he also had essential thrombocythaemia. The bone marrow was producing too many red platelets which was very dangerous and could cause blood clotting in many parts of the body. This meant a lifetime of tablets to take to keep the red platelet levels down. He soon became an interesting patient with the rarity of his two complaints. Trust it to be my husband. I often told him he wasn't normal. We struggled through months and months in and out of hospital with David having blood tests, the drawing of blood and regular visits to see Dr Freeman, which held such trepidation. We were so frequently in the Edward Jenner Ward that we became known by our Christian names. David tried in the meantime to keep himself in peak condition: cycling, walking, and joining the Bristol Community Trust over 50s Walking Football Club. He bought a chest expander which he used twice daily.

*

In the October we decided to decorate the dining room and David and I moved some furniture. After that he was moaning and groaning about straining his arm and added he had aching pains in his shoulder. He tried rubbing in different anti-inflammatory creams but to no avail. I commented that I moved the furniture as well but my arms weren't aching. Such a thoughtless thing to say, but sometimes stupid things tumble from my mouth before putting my brain into action. He huffed at me. I took the hint and tossed him one of my looks.

Then the merry-go-round of life became very serious. One morning David marched into the bedroom where I was laying in bed (I sensed a seriousness that instantly seized me. My stomach somersaulted, which over the course of time I learnt to get used to). 'I have this lump the size of a golf ball at the side of my neck. I think it's my thyroid. Feel it, feel it.' I sat bolt upright in bed and felt the lump. I knew instantly it was something really serious. He made a phone call to our local surgery and within an hour he was at the doctors' and another blood test was taken. The doctor checked around his neck for other swellings. We then waited. Sure enough, two days later, and too quickly we sensed, we were summoned to the hospital where further tests were taken. The doctor told us it was a tumour and half of his thyroid gland would need to be removed. This was the beginning of a lifetime of tablets to adjust David's thyroid levels.

*

Back we went to hospital the following week with David's bag of clothes. He was prepared for the operation and a large arrow was drawn on the side of the neck to show where they had to operate. I waved cheerily to David with my painted clown's face on as he was whisked away on a trolley. Quoting William Wordsworth, "I wandered lonely as a cloud" (but could not see the daffodils) down the long corridors of the hospital and departed from the building.

My heart had picked up its pace and was beating rapidly outside of myself which made me feel quite shaky. I squeezed myself into my little red Citroen C1 car and snaked my way back home in the snarling traffic. I kept my eyes firmly on the road but my mind was flowing in a different direction. I telephoned in the afternoon to see if he was out of theatre and later went to visit him with my daughter. David's face lit up as we entered the ward. I glanced at my daughter and studied her lopsided frozen smile and knotted brow. I could see her desperately fighting back tears as she gazed at her dad laying there with tubes coming out of his thyroid, and other places. I leaned towards the daylight in my mind, and tried to lighten the atmosphere by cheerfully saying, 'That's another fine mess you've got yourself into.' It was stupid and ridiculous, but by then my brain had become scrambled. We made light trivial conversation with David and departed.

At home, being a night owl, I made my way late in the evening to an empty bed and lay down with thoughts racing through my head. I so wanted David and left the bedroom door ajar for him, but I knew he would only appear in my dreams. They had taken a biopsy of the tumour at the hospital and we would have the long wait to find out the results. My daughter wanted to come with me and her dad when they gave us the diagnosis to hear the information herself.

*

David arrived home after a few days and a week later the three of us entered the specialist's office for the results of the biopsy. I immediately clocked there was a nurse present in the background. Being hypersensitive I knew in my mind that it was a horrible sign. I tried to quickly read the language in the specialist's eyes, but to no avail. We were then told the tumour in the thyroid was cancerous and they needed to check the rest of his body and take a PET/CT (positron emission tomography and computed tomography) scan which would take place at the Cheltenham Cobalt Imaging Centre (which is the only imaging centre in the country). They put radioactive fluorine into the body plus sugar. This travels around the system and the solution pitches where there are cancerous cells which show up as lights by the scanning process.

When we eventually attended our appointment a few weeks later we found out it was a long process, including the waiting, and you have to snuff out half a day. David became very chilled lying still in the machine and was quite wobbly when he left the centre. He had driven his Saab automatic car but it landed on me to get us back. I had not driven an automatic or the Saab so I had to concentrate, take the bull by the horns and get us home. I have a hopeless sense of direction and sometimes I travel the wrong way even with the satellite navigation, so David between his huffs and puffs had to talk me home, as well as feeling lightheaded.

We were called yet again to the Gloucestershire Royal Hospital for the results of the scan. We were taken into a room, David, my daughter and I. The specialist was waiting quietly, shuffling and reshuffling his paperwork and glancing at the computer screen before him. This time David was seated in a big chair. The chair was a replica of the chair in *Mastermind* and the same colour. It was very stark and had an aura of impending doom about it. A nurse was perched, like a bird on a branch, in the corner of the room. I felt wobbly but tried to control my emotions. We were told as gently as we could by Dr Freeman that David had cancer in his plasma, which was circulating around his body, and a big patch of cancer had taken hold in the clavicle. That explained the pain in his shoulder when moving the furniture. There was also a tiny grouping of cancer on his spine and a little spot on his rib. David took a deep breath and absorbed the news as best he could. He began asking questions. My daughter put on her teacher's hat. I was so grateful that she could sensibly discuss the way forward as I had turned to mush and felt quite nauseous. I found the word cancer was a hard word to chew on and could not swallow it. I then proceeded to let my family down by bursting into torrents of tears. The nurse kindly passed me a box of tissues. I knew immediately in my heart I would have to learn to toughen up to deflect all the hard knocks that life was going to hurl at me. After the diagnosis, which I think we all knew and were dreading, we made our way home.

I began to question my faith. What kind of god would give David cancer? Nevertheless, I made sure I prayed in earnest that night and every night thereafter for David, as he didn't pray. I was taking no chances. I needed God on my side. I also visited St Arilda's Church in Oldbury-on-Severn searching for an inner peace. Alone in the church I pleaded with God for his strength and mercy to pull David through. I suddenly sensed His presence and felt for that short period of time a fleeting calmness. I left one of my poems as a thank you for that moment of peace in the church, and hoped people would reflect on the words. The vicar later pinned my poem to the notice board at the entrance of the church for all the parishioners to read.

I visited a so-called lifelong friend a few days later to give her the news about David. I broke down in tears in her house as I needed a shoulder to cry on and couldn't let David see again how wretched I felt. Her husband strolled into the lounge and told me he didn't want crying in his home. The silence drained from my mouth. How you get to know people!

*

A regime of chemotherapy began in earnest, regular trips to the Edward Jenner Ward in Gloucestershire Royal Hospital on Fridays and sometimes days in between if there was a problem. David felt sick after his treatments and suffered flu-like symptoms which took a hold on the weekend and then he would recover as best he could during the week. Along with anti-sickness tablets and tablets for his thyroid, steroid tablets had to be taken. After steroid tablets David had a lot of painful cramps which found him leaping from the bed and cursing (the cramps still continue to this day). They were in his legs, feet and hands. The first time he took the steroid tablets he had to take forty-two in a plastic cup after chemotherapy treatment along with all his other pills. Having an aversion to any tablets, even aspirin, he was horrified, but it had to be done. He hesitantly stared into the cup and the stones cast their barbarous eyes back at him. The battle had commenced. One tablet he took during the course of time he had terrible trouble to swallow; he used to retch. He tried all sorts to help him swallow the pill, for example, blanketing it in bread, but to no avail. After weeks we found the tablet should have been dissolved in water. How stupid! We must remember to read all the instructions carefully. After months of chemotherapy and pills for all his ailments, we were going to have to endure two years of travelling to and fro to the hospital for David to have steroid drips to build up his bones due to the damage caused by the cancer. One positive result from the cancer was the doctors decided to take no more blood for his hemochromatosis as cancer was far more serious and the doctors concentrated on that. Also, they said, forget the foraging for food to eat

12

without iron because David's body needed all the nutrients it could get, and for me to feed him with nothing but the best.

With regular visits to the Dracula Ward, I became an expert at looking into faces of couples and working out who the poorly one was. Their faces would have a yellow pallor or fifty shades of grey. There were sometimes women with brightly coloured scarves wrapped around their heads, yet again awaiting more chemotherapy. The grandchildren told David that if his hair began falling out they would arrive with an electric razor and shave his head for him. It was a way for them to lighten the situation and get involved, which was essential. David, luckily, kept all of his beautiful silver grey curls and did not need a wig. Zoe, our daughter, contacted the grandchildren's schools as they were getting quite distressed by grampy's illness. The cancer was snaking its way through all of the family.

One day a middle-aged couple appeared from the specialist's room and sat awaiting treatment after their discussion with the doctor. The woman buried her head in her husband's shoulder, shielding her face from the incoming storm and sobbed silently, dabbing her eyes now and then with a tissue. I wanted to wrap my arms around her but could not; after all, I was British, stiff upper lip and all that. Her husband, frozen in time, stared un-movingly ahead, obviously trying to focus on what he had heard. My heart went out to them; I felt so helpless but could not give succour as David and I had our own problems to deal with, as did most of us in that room.

We became permanent fixtures in the Edward Jenner Ward, week after week, month after month. Sometimes it would be quite empty, but more often than not it would be quite full and we would have to stand like tin soldiers with our backs to the wall. There was this fatty chair for obese people in the centre of the room, always empty. I would look at my husband and point to it, but we would dare not sit on its lap like overripe lovers, although we could both squash into its arms. We felt we would appear rude. The chair, taking up space, would defiantly scorn at us and grinned with its cold plastic smirk as we stood wilting in the crowded room. There were the odd obese people but mostly in wheelchairs so they did not need the fatty chair. Sometimes I was allowed, with David, into the chemotherapy room to see a doctor, or sometimes not. It was a pleasant enough room although the patients had cancer. Nurses would bustle around with all their gloves, aprons and other protective gear on in case there was a spillage of the dangerous chemicals that were being dripped into the patients. Patients would all be sat in soft chairs wired up to their drips, some watching the television. The bleepers would continually go off, signalling the bags had been drained of their poison. A lady with a trolley would wander around giving patients succour, sandwiches, and tea which was often needed. Sometimes I would pop in with a chai latte from the coffee shop for David and hold his hand. How brave he was. I had to remind myself through the depths of winter that spring was not far behind.

I was given mountains of paperwork concerning people to contact to assist us, if needed, such as the Carers Trust, the Myeloma Support Group, McMillan Nurses, Crossroads etc., but ridiculously I tried to continue down my stony path alone, only once telephoning an organisation to talk to someone for support when I hit rock bottom. The woman on the other end was pleasant enough but seemed to be lacking in compassion. Her words broke into a mist in my mind listening to her tongue without tone. She repeated the same words of sympathy in monotone she had obviously rehearsed time and time again. Maybe it was a bad day for her. I did eventually receive kindness from some of the organisations associated with cancer through the course of time. Often support groups would hold their meetings, for instance, on the second Tuesday in the month or third Thursday in the month etc., and because my mind was so scrambled I could not absorb all the times of the meetings and venues, and could not be bothered to jot them down on my calendar. Daggy me!

*

After months of weekly sessions at the hospital and gruelling treatment, we found David's cancer had cleared and he was in remission. Oh, the happiness. Our broad smiles dwelt a little longer on our faces. More tears from David and I, but they were the waters of joy that sprung from the rejuvenated fountain of life. We could begin our lives again in earnest. David and I joined different clubs, went out as much as we could and enjoyed living. He was chairman of the BMW Motorbike Club and also belonged to the Triumph Motorbike Club. He continued with the Bristol Community Trust over 50s Walking Football Club and the quizzes held afterwards, which he enjoyed. He then decided to assist with the Berkeley Steam Preservation Society and began putting in place and writing all their health and safety plans and reports as health and safety was his vocation with British Petroleum before he retired.

David was having regular checks at Cheltenham Cobalt Imaging Centre, then suddenly alarm bells. After twelve months' remission we were told they'd found five minute lights. Action stations again. We found ourselves once again speedily travelling towards our fears. They decided on another scan two months later to check on the lights. Two had shrunk, two had remained the same and one had grown. They felt there was a need to take a biopsy of the larger light. Weeks and weeks in limbo, we waited patiently for an appointment. The time span awaiting the biopsy had always held a concern for us because we marked time for so long. Were we lost in the winding corridors of the system or not? We would never know. We wondered if we had not been notified about our appointment as the specialists felt the tumour would not grow rapidly and there was no urgency. Dizzied by apprehension, it was like living with a time bomb.

Finally we had an appointment, and two weeks before the biopsy I noticed David was drinking lots and lots of water. I asked him if he was all right and he replied with words sharply polished that he was. David slowly became snappy through the fear of his illness, which was understandable. I noticed there was something not quite right with his pallor. He always had a slight flush due to his high levels of iron, but his complexion had taken on a worrying tinge. My daughter spotted it and remarked, but he flippantly shrugged it off. By the time Friday arrived I queried with him again whether he was well? He told me that his water was dark brown and could I look at it. To my horror it was. I told him to phone the doctor immediately. The doctor asked him if it was an emergency for that day and like a fool he said no, and he was not in any pain. By Saturday, concerned, David decided to take a sample of his urine to our local hospital. Immediately they referred him to Accident and Emergency at Gloucestershire Royal Hospital. Off we went to a place which at the best of times is horrendous but definitely not a nice place to visit on the weekend. It was like visiting the café at the end of the universe in the film *Star Wars*. Young and old, people covered in blood splashes, coughs being happily distributed between everybody. Shapes and forms wearily huddled over cardboard sick bowls. After hours of patiently waiting, he was placed on a bed, blood pressure taken, and wired to a heart monitor. He explained his symptoms to the nurse who looked at him with only a pinprick of concern. She immediately told him to remove his shirt. Shock upon shock, he was yellow; he had jaundice. Being a man of little words, he had not said. I hadn't gazed at his body because it being winter he always had his day clothes or his pyjamas on. Then it dawned on me why he had looked so peculiar: his skin and eyes were yellow! That was it; he was staying in hospital. No ifs and buts; something was malfunctioning in his body. He was then moved into four different temporary available beds around the hospital, finally finishing in the Kidney/Liver Ward although it was cancer causing all the problems. It became musical beds, not chairs. Nobody knew where to put him. He travelled the well-trodden tracks of the wards on a trolley. I drove home to get him all his toiletries and clothes, returned to the hospital, stayed with him a while and then made my way back. I arrived home late and crawled like a crab into an empty bed yet again holding on to my teddy bear (at nearly sixty-eight years of age, crazy!) and wondered what was going wrong. My life was out of control and spiralling downwards like a corkscrew. I was now spending so much time in the hospital it was becoming a second home to me.

In amongst all the mayhem I was endeavouring to take an Open University degree, and was studying between his treatments hunched over my books, revising in the Costa

Coffee shop at the hospital. Two years of "Creative Writing", one year of "Arts Past and Present" and then "Psychology". The staff in the coffee shop looked pitifully at me and I knew suddenly how narrow my life had become when one young assistant said, 'Black Americano again?' They knew me all too well. I would, believe it or not, get excited if the coffee shop supplied my favourite chocolate mallow teacake. I would sit in my torment alone, sometimes lifting my gaze from my books and staring at all the characters in the coffee shop. There would be obese young girls in their onesies and portable drips, probably escaping for an hour from their wards to munch through a chocolate brownie. Maybe they were desperate to escape from the bland alabaster hospital food. Elderly people, older than God, in wheelchairs, were being pushed by their spouses who could hardly walk themselves. Doctors would huddle together at tables in the coffee shop, male and female bonding. It was obvious by the seriousness of their faces they were discussing patients. The young male doctors always dressed the same; you could pick them out. Smart trousers, shirts with the top buttons undone, often sleeves slightly rolled up. Their names pinned to their shirts also gave the game away. The name tabs, maybe, were not only to assist the patients but to tell them who they were after a staggering fourteen-hour shift. I noticed two scruffy young parents with a baby in a beaten-up, mud-splattered pram. The young man, who you would not trust near your handbag, dived into the pram and produced a baby like a rabbit from a magician's hat. The baby boy looked about four months old, and I could not believe it, he had the same unwashed joggers on as his dad, and just as stained. The father grabbed a bottle from the pram, shook it and commenced to feed the baby who by then was ravenous. He kissed the baby gently on the head which sobered me up. I felt embarrassed by my first impression of the young man. *Never judge a book by its cover* instantly sprang to mind. The mother sat motionless with her greasy, lank dark hair dropping in her eyes and continued gazing at her iPad, obviously transfixed by what her mates were texting, probably about their nights out and what colour lipstick they had just bought and who had dumped who. Or maybe she was too wrapped up in her *Angry Birds* game, and lost in her virtual reality world. She made no attempt to bond with her baby.

I continued visiting David every afternoon and marched up and down the long corridors punctuated by many different varieties of walking sticks and aged people. My daughter and her family visited David every night. I preferred, being cowardly, the afternoon visits as I did not like driving alone at night, although being winter I still drove home in semi-darkness. They kept David wired up and did more tests. By then his stools had turned black (we later found out this was due to him bleeding internally). They also realised David was anaemic. The only good thing about one of David's ailments was that his hemochromatosis had helped to counterbalance the anaemia. Alas, another satanic beast, blacker than black, was ready to spring from life's forest. The doctors arranged for David to have more scans and found to their horror that he had nine cunning multiple plasmacytoma cancers, and that the one the size of a tennis ball had blocked the entrance to his pancreas. The others in the flesh on his back were the size of marbles. He had to have another emergency operation whereby they put a biliary stent into the entrance of the pancreas. David had obstructive jaundice and biliary sepsis due to the pancreatic head plasmacytoma. He then had two weeks of Hell in a ward with five other men in the tower block of the hospital. The old concrete tower block's exterior was stark and chilled the bone, although its heart pulsated with the warmth of the nursing staff. Amongst the teasing stars, the tower block reminded me of a dying man's taupe finger pointing desperately to the heavens above, searching for hope.

David had a bad reaction to the stent and had to be put on an antibiotic drip. He then had a bad reaction to the cannula; his hand turned to fiery shades of red and purple like rich over-ripe autumn berries, so they had to transfer the cannula to the other hand. His liver and kidneys malfunctioned and he had to be put on another drip to flush them out. The doctors were very concerned that the cancer had spread to those vital organs. Because of all the problems and fluid retention, his stomach swelled up like a balloon. He looked like a Womble. It was such a worrying time. My inner vision was becoming scarred. My stomach had gotten used to doing somersaults, and some days I felt so tense all my food was flowing through me like the rushing of the tides. I felt lost, and could not find myself. I was bubble wrapped in fearful thoughts of what would happen if things got worse. Days in the hospital were scattered with many emergencies. I got the lowdown on all the patients when visiting David. The food in the hospital was pallid and unappetising which did not help the situation as David needed all the nutrients he could get. Where had all the colours gone? Although his appetite had disappeared he was pleading with me to take extra food in, which I did. The nurses were kind but rushed off their feet. It seemed to be the patients that caused a lot of the trouble. One man in the ward wouldn't let the others open the windows for fresh air and complained he was cold. One night all the patients' temperatures were raised. The nurse on duty could not fathom it out. David told her it was because everyone was too hot due to the windows being shut. She immediately flung them open. Also, a few other rows sparked off. One telling the other he was tired of hearing about his life and the other telling him to shut up. Some of the patients spoke to the nurses rudely which upset David even more as he knew they were doing their best under such extenuating circumstances. I visited him on one occasion whereby a fight had broken out between father and son (who was the patient). The son wanted his dad to bring his five-year-old son in, but the father refused and told his son he was a waste of space and that he was not fit to have a child. A lot of swearing ensued. David, depressed and wired up to drips, began to sob loudly. It broke my heart but my suffering at that time was too deep for tears. I immediately pulled the curtains around him so he could not see anything that was happening. David desperately wanted to go home which made me feel so powerless. The young man pulled the curtains back to apologise. I told him in no uncertain terms the patients did not want to witness arguments as they were all very ill. I was so consumed by my overflowing broth of anger. I wanted to shout and shout at him to vent my spleen but knew my words would be immaterial and would have been meaningless to the dull ear.

One light-hearted incident occurred when David saw a man walking past his window on the ledge outside. He nearly had a fit. As he was in a ward seven floors up he thought it was a Jumper! He said his heart skipped a beat. Thankfully it was the window cleaner. He later saw the thin safety wire securely strapped to his back.

*

Day after day I watched David suffer in the ward but could not take him home. David and I were both caged, he in the ward, and me caged by his cancer. Neither of us could find the rusty keys to escape. Each day I passed young and old hovering at the entrance of the hospital in their scruffy pyjamas, and fluffy slippers on their feet, which resembled dank defeated dogs. They all seemed to have drips in one hand and a fag in the other. The sad clowns, puffing away, huddled together shivering in the biting winter air and peered at me through their greasy hair. One, covered in tattoos, was scoffing a packet of Quavers and stood guard over his bottle of Coke on the rain swept concrete. Not Diet Coke, but the bottle packed to capacity with plentiful spoonfuls of sugar. *Good diet there*, I silently told myself, but I suppose it was their lives not mine, so it was up to them if they wanted to kill themselves. Why did they abuse their bodies, why didn't they realise the most precious thing they had in their pathetic lives was their health? Depression and hopelessness hung heavy like a weighty cumulus cloud above their heads. I wanted to shake and shake them but I knew it would be useless.

We waited day upon day desperate for the occasional visit from the specialists. They were really compassionate people who had to cover so many patients. We realised it was as hard for them as it was for us. We listened intently for any branches of hope we could cling to, no matter how slight, and held on to them by our fingernails as best we could.

In between all the hospital visits I was trying to deal with all the clubs David belonged to. We had organised a weekend away to Bournemouth for eighty people from the BMW Motorbike Club and all the calls were coming in for me to check whether people's rooms had been reserved, and cheques were arriving thick and fast which had to be posted to the treasurer. Prizes to go to Bournemouth were lined up in my hall. David was producing health and safety reports for the Berkeley Steam Train Society which had to be in and was arranging meetings. There were also some calls from his over 50s Walking Football Club. When I arrived home every evening I would be greeted by a green light flashing on the telephone telling me dozens of messages had been left. I would then have to reply to them. One night after staggering in from hospital on a cold, dank evening, I was greeted by a call from a woman flapping about whether her room was still booked at the hotel in Bournemouth. I really had to keep my cool. I was also struggling with my Open University revision, and my examinations were looming once again.

Two weeks in hospital, the only visitors David had were me, my daughter and her family, and one loyal friend and partner. The five weeks in hospital throughout his ordeals, we were his only visitors. I felt such anger as I was continually telephoning people amongst the incoming calls to tell them where David was, but obviously people had too many commitments like having their hair done, shopping at Tesco, or going to the pub, to visit David and to relieve me for a day, or even pick me up to give me a break from driving. Illness did not fit into their social calendars. I knew I shouldn't get angry but I did, and my eyes continually leaked. I was Mrs Angry. There were husbands who were so controlled by their wives that they could not make the trip alone to see their friend. I was shocked by some of the so-called lifelong friends and others who had taken cover and did not want to get involved. Maybe they were too miserly to put petrol in their cars to visit David. I was later told by a social worker who came to visit me that I had to make allowances for people not bothering to visit David as many people did not like visiting hospitals, and illness frightened them. What a weak excuse that was. *That's fine*, I thought. I do not like hospitals or illness but I recalled all the people I had visited in hospitals in the past, and I made a vow to myself there and then that no matter what happened in the future I would not be visiting anybody again in hospital except for my own family and those that gave us comfort. It cuts both ways. However, I did have a couple of friends who, unable to visit with their husbands because of their own family health problems, gave succour over the telephone regularly which was greatly appreciated. They were the odd few who stood up to the mark.

My loyal friends Colin and Avril (whom I mentioned previously) bless them, who did visit David, offered to bring David home with me when he was discharged from hospital. We got David from his ward and sat with him and his bag of clothes in the hospital coffee shop waiting for the mountain of tablets to take home from the pharmacy. Four hours later we were still waiting for the paperwork to be processed by the ward and taken to the pharmacy. David, by then, had slumped over the table and had turned as grey as the day outside. He could not manage one more chai latte; he just wanted to get home. My friends had been through the process with their first partners who had died, and knew what was entailed waiting for prescriptions. I cannot thank them enough for their time and effort. We watched comings and goings in the coffee shop. I watched the queues of people waiting for their takeaway coffees and cakes, which were mainly (I could tell by their uniforms) the people who worked in the hospital who had no time to sit down. I stared at the queue of hospital visitors waiting patiently, and the slow process of making the coffee. My mind wandered and in my head I reorganised the system in the coffee shop to make it more efficient. Oh, if I was younger and in charge, things would be so different. The customer always came first in my world. Although the assistants were very friendly, there seemed to be a lack of hands to the deck.

David and I finally got dropped off at home in the dark. The look of relief on my husband's face said it all. He sighed as he sunk into his reclining chair, happily cupped in that moment of peace. 'Don't ever let me go into that lunatic asylum again,' he groaned. But that was not going to be the case.

Eventually my faith in humanity began to be restored. A few faithful friends arrived from the BMW Motorbike Club, and also Alan from the Bristol City over 50s Walking Football Club. Alan brought much appreciated flowers, books and biscuits. Our new neighbours Sam and Barbara in their eighties (without me asking) mowed our front lawns and bought me flowers, which was so generous and kind. Our window cleaner and friend who lived nearby kept his mobile phone on by his bedside so he could rush David to the Accident and Emergency department with me if needed. I had been told by a specialist that if calling 999 it can take a while for assistance and it might well be best to take David straight to hospital myself in an emergency. David is such a big man for me to manage that I knew I would have required assistance.

We had a peaceful week home. I continued to keep my life as normal as possible under such extenuating circumstances. I still had my grandchildren and daughter over for tea on Thursdays. That was my joy as the grandchildren breathed life back into my home. I still took my mother for her weekly trip to The Mall. I had to give my ninety-year-old mother a day of my time. Wearily, I am of the generation that was brought up to believe you have to do everything for your parents as they are the most important people in your life and you come second. Whether or not they did anything for you in their lives is another matter. I married at nineteen years of age and deserted the nest just before my mother divorced my father. The younger generation, rightly so, believe they have their own lives to live and follow their beliefs. My generation, the baby boomers, are sandwiched between two different ideologies and give to both generations without expecting assistance from anybody if they can help it. From my perspective, and watching my friends of the same age, we baby boomers endeavour to give a slice of ourselves to everyone if we can, but we must remember, however, to keep a slice just for us. I felt a wave of selfishness wash over me again and blushed at my thoughts. Where was the familiar person I greeted in the mirror every day; where had the smiling face hurled from Heaven disappeared to? The usual chirpy fun type of person had been snuffed out in a puff of smoke. Gone was the light.

*

Sunday: A couple from our BMW Motorbike Club came to visit us. They departed, making their way to the AGM in Wales. Half an hour later David came down the stairs more ashen-faced than usual. He told me his manly parts had blown up like a balloon and could I take a look. Long time, no see, I thought. It had been ages since I'd viewed them, as bodily fluid (intercourse) was a no-no when taking chemotherapy, unless of course a condom was worn (which David and I were well out of practice using), or jokingly you wanted to turn green and lose all your teeth from the poison! I was stunned by what I saw. His manly parts were twice the size they should be and his penis resembled a huge funghi mushroom. I knew it was something serious and that it was not because he was excited to see me. My stomach somersaulted into another world. I asked if it was sore to pass water and he replied, 'No.' I phoned the hospital's emergency number I had been given, to be told to telephone my doctor's emergency number, which I did. After a time endlessly pressing numbers on my telephone, an answerphone told me to telephone 111. I found myself spinning round and round in circles chasing my tail, while trying to explain all the complications to anyone who would listen, and an indifferent doctor on 111 getting impatient with me. One thing I tried desperately not to do was argue with him, but he was not me and could not comprehend the problems I was facing with all of David's ailments. Alas we ended up having the mother of all rows. I could not get hold of friends to help me with David as most of them were at the BMW Motorbike Sunday meeting in Wales, so I took the bull by the horns and telephoned my son-in-law who raced from a rugby meeting to take David and I to our local hospital. We met our daughter there. I needed assistance as David was feeling very weak and could not, with a forced gait, walk very far. We all amassed and helped David to a chair. I refused to keep David with cancer in the waiting room for long, amongst all the coughing and spluttering and illnesses, and told the receptionist in no uncertain manner. The doctor, who had been tipped off that we were agitated, saw us as quickly as he could, which was admirable as I was slowly losing the will to live. The doctor was confused by the swelling in David's penis as fluid retention would normally be in the legs. He checked his lower limbs and found a reddish-purple bruise snaking up the inside of David's left leg. We were informed, because it was Sunday, there were no nurses to administer blood tests, so we were told to take an emergency letter from him to our local doctor first thing Monday morning for David to have blood tests. The conclusion from this is never to be poorly on a weekend.

*

Monday: I duly did what I was told and pushed myself to the front of the queue at our local doctors', refusing once again to put David in the doctors' waiting room with all the dangerous micro-organisms. They reluctantly gave us a room on our own. After examining David's leg, the doctor told us to make an emergency journey to Gloucestershire Royal Hospital Accident and Emergency Department as the doctor was positive David had deep vein thrombosis. I threw him straight into the car and telephoned my brother for help as my son-in-law was in Slough and my daughter was in Newport having her hair dyed. I garbled out orders for him to get to Gloucestershire Royal Hospital as it was an emergency and I needed his help to handle David. John, my brother, was, in fact, in Southmead Hospital with his wife who was on a magnesium drip which she has to have frequently. He left her stranded on her drip and raced to the hospital where we were. Jokingly, she told me that I still owe her for a perm as she had to catch the bus back home in the rain!

By the time I arrived at the hospital David was so frail I left him in the car and ran to the reception desk searching for a wheelchair. I was told a man at the desk to quickly grab the last one in the corner before anybody else took it. It was a cumbersome, ugly chair with a blue vinyl seat like something from the 1940s. I was told it was so heavy it would be best to pull it, not push it. The rotund man behind the reception desk made no attempt to assist me. He smirked as he watched me manoeuvre the wheelchair (I tossed him one of my withering looks) and eventually struggled helplessly with it, dragging it backwards into the car park and, exhausted, dumped my husband like a sack of spuds onto its lap. The wheelchair had a mind of its own, like a shopping trolley, but after a while (me being five feet two inches and hubby being six feet three inches) I got him into the Accident and Emergency Department. By now David was a deathly grey and slumped forward in the chair like Quasimodo. He had become so exhausted, and what with of his drugs he was on, he was not making much sense and his speech had slurred. We were taken from the Accident and Emergency Department and told to queue in a corridor. All the beds were taken and there was a row of trolleys down the long alleyway with sick people on them waiting patiently for their turn. Old and young, and most holding tightly on to their cardboard sick bowls. I heard there was an epidemic of norovirus in the wards. Some wards had been closed down. Fear had taken hold again; that was the last thing David needed. A row broke out between a patient and a receptionist. The patient felt he had waited too long for assistance from the doctors, so the security officers were called. It was quite a raucous affair. Sometimes the National Health Service gets abused which is terribly sad as they do their best under such extenuating circumstances.

My brother eventually arrived and I could see the shock on his face as he looked at David. I asked the nurses at reception if my brother and I could have chairs to sit on as we would probably have to wait a long time. The nurses looked contemptuously at me for interrupting their conversations, and said curtly there were none available. No chairs! I was not willing to stand for what could be hours. Anger exploded within me. I proceeded to march down two corridors until I found an empty waiting room with the door slammed shut to visitors. I entered and then struggled up and back twice to my husband with two armchairs, one chair for me, and one for my brother. The strength needed to do that even amazed me. It must have been the adrenalin pumping through my veins. I could see the annoyance and irritation on the faces of the whispering nurses and receptionists, as, they leant over the desk to see what I was up to. *Let them come and make my day*, I thought. They knew better than that as I was in battle mode, and attempted to busy themselves.

After the experience with the hospital wheelchair I decided to use my ninety-year-old mother's collapsible wheelchair and kept it in my car as she only suffers a little from arthritis now and again and does not really need it. She did not protest, thank goodness.

Finally, after hours of waiting, David got a bed in the Acute Ward. By then he was quite incoherent through feeling weak. A nurse asked David if he wanted a cup of tea to which he replied, 'Yes, please.' An hour and a half later the tea had not arrived. Afraid to leave his side, I kept asking where it was but felt I was becoming a nuisance. Hey ho! The doctors eventually checked his limbs, measured his calves and the upper part of his legs and informed us it was very serious as they were confident at that precise time that he did have deep vein thrombosis. One leg was bigger than the other. After putting cameras down him previously, and finding he was bleeding internally and had lost two pints of blood, they decided they could not give him a blood-thinning drip or tablets. My brother and I looked at each other; the silence spoke volumes. My brother kept going in and out of the curtains around David's bed as he did not know what to do or say. I was so grateful he was with me, although he was as much use as a button on a begging plate, bless him! I knew how he felt as my brother and I were ridiculously reacting the same way. My daughter arrived and this gave my brother the opportunity to make his way home. My daughter listened to the specialist and was told the same as me. I asked what would happen if the blood clot moved. He told us if it travelled to the lungs (known as a PE, pulmonary embolism) David would hit the ground. The staff, I could see were very concerned. Luckily enough, David, feeling so frail, realised little of what was going on around him. I glanced across to my daughter and scanned her face. Her father's inherited frown appeared and scuttled across her brow, and her jaw locked tightly. I realised immediately the seriousness of the moment and asked the specialist if my daughter and I could speak to him privately and then proceeded to ask him if we should get Richard my son back from Australia. He said it had to be our decision as it was not up to him to comment. My daughter and I looked at one another and read our minds. We immediately made the decision to get him home. We felt if we did not, and a tragedy happened, Rick might never forgive us for not telephoning sooner. We made the call and, bless him he was on a plane within four hours, travelling back across the world. Unbeknown to us he had a bag packed in Australia in case he had to make an emergency dash. We had kept him informed about his dad by Skype.

My daughter picked him up from Heathrow, drove him to my home and Rick and I made our way to hospital. David became emotional and sobbed tears of joy in the ward to see Richard. I noticed the light of love shine brightly in David's eyes. Rick, I felt, was shocked by David's appearance, and seeing him so weak and wired up to drips in the ward was not a good sight. I picked up on Rick's sharp intake of breath. Everything, it seemed, in David's body, by then, was not working properly. We all waited with baited breath to see what would happen next, but thank the Lord the blood clots did not move to the lungs. One of the blood clots had settled itself deeply into his calf which was later discovered by another scan. I felt doctors had their work cut out as they were trying to find which veins the blood clots were in. As the day came to a close, I took Rick back home. We reached the A38 and, alas, found ourselves gridlocked as a motorcyclist had had a nasty accident. The police and the ambulance service had arrived. Rick sprung out of the car to see what was going on and returned to tell me a motorcyclist was lying motionless in the middle of the road. Poor Rick had travelled across the world, seen his very sick dad in hospital and had now witnessed a terrible accident. He said he was totally numb and could not feel any emotion. He said if someone put a gun to his head he would not care; they could shoot him! As we were stuck fast and could not turn the car around, it took us an hour and a half to cover what was normally a thirty-minute drive.

*

Later on in the week eight specialists held a meeting to decide what to do with David as his case was so complicated. They decided, because he was so poorly, that they needed to start his chemotherapy treatment immediately as they could not wait any longer. David was desperate to leave the hospital so they gave him another day in the ward where they put him on a steroid drip to build him up strong enough to take chemotherapy the following day. They then told me to take David home in his wheelchair as he was so depressed, and to bring him back the following day (on Friday).

*

Friday: My son, daughter and I took David seated in the wheelchair, back again in his pyjamas and dressing gown, to the Edward Jenner Ward. We passed the receptionist we knew well and who knew David. She smiled and said, 'Hello.' I caught her out of the corner of my eye and as she swung around to stare once again at David's face, I clocked her vexed expression and read her thoughts. David was shown to a seat in the Chemotherapy Ward. His ankles had swollen to twice the size they should be and he stared at the ground with a look of defeat on his emaciated ashen face. The specialist entered the room and David gamut of emotions took hold and he broke down. He felt he could not go on and that he was totally out of control of his life and wanted to be once again the man of the house. It took all three of us and the doctor an hour to talk him around to continue with the chemotherapy. Gentle cajoling by the doctor saved the day; the doctor was so kind and held David's hand. David got through a box of tissues before he could proceed with the treatment, and once again, as usual, had to place his hand in a bowl of warm water to raise the veins ready for the needle.

My son and I finally got David home after a traumatic day. Everyone was so exhausted. I sat deflated on the settee while David slept in his chair and my son slept on the settee. It was like "Sleepy Hollow". I listened quietly to the gentle music of their breathing. I later put on my computer to see if there were any important emails. Suddenly I spotted an email from author John Holland who was also the judge of a short story competition I had entered. Apparently, I had got through to the final twenty and John had sent the email to tell me how much he had enjoyed my story even though I did not win. Suddenly a ray of light shone brightly in my darkened tunnel. I replied to tell him how much he had lifted my spirits and to thank him. Sadly, I was not able to attend the Stroud Writers' Circle monthly meetings which I cherished as I knew I could not leave David alone, and alas, my brain had become as dry as a desert and my creative juices were not flowing fast through the deep trenches of my mind. However, I still clung to my pen knowing at a later date I would write again; it is my life's blood. I had to also contact my tutor and the support group from the Open University to halt the course I was on, as I found myself one day staring at my computer and books and realised I could not absorb a thing. My nails were bitten and pared to the quick and tears drizzled down my face and plopped onto my psychology *Investigating Methods* book. My tutor and the support team were very sympathetic and stopped my course for me, which I can continue when ready. Will I ever be prepared? I had no idea what lay in front of me on this long journey. The specialist told me that 'IF' the treatment worked we would have a window of opportunity to continue as normal. How long that window would be both David and I had no idea. Would it be two months, twelve months, two years? Nobody knew. We understood then we had to re-evaluate our lives. Would David be able to lift his motorbike and ride again, for instance? I knew I could not broach that delicate subject with him and take away his freedom. Deep down inside I thought I knew, but how lovely it would be to be proved wrong.

David finally learnt how to scale the stairs cautiously, leaning forward in case he collapsed so he could venture up and down to bed. Being a person with DSPD (Delayed Sleep Phase Disorder), I would follow him when he retired to bed and watch him sleeping throughout the long nights while keeping the eye at the back of my head on him and listening to his breathing. Before David went to sleep he would line some of his tablets up on the kitchen worktop and some by his bed. He had beforehand methodically produced spreadsheets on what to take, and when. The nurses at the hospital when he began his treatment had all assembled to see his spreadsheets. They said they had never seen such detailed charts and were very impressed. He had thought he was out of control but I could see that was not the case. Just doing that small thing had revealed a glimmer of his former self.

Each day at home he would move from his bed to his reclining chair by the patio doors and study the trees and birds and squirrels etc. How he enjoyed sitting quietly, absorbing the peace and to watch nature unfold, untouched by the sorrows of man. It was so therapeutic for him. He was relieved to be at home. We could view the news on the television or anything too depressing. The films had to be as light as a feather and cheerful. We both had no energy for anything else. Even when I was in the car on my own I could not listen to music, especially love songs, or I would burst into tears. I kept bumping my head against the dark, dank walls of my fears. The old workhorse had been well and truly beaten and was not in a good place.

*

Over the following weeks I watched David's weight plummet. Trapped in the snares of cancer, he began to waste away. I noticed when he undressed the muscles had disappeared at the top of his legs and his flesh dropped in folds like creased linen hanging from a washing line on a becalmed day. His face had shrunk slightly, although a gentle powdering of haemachromatosis pink rouge had found its place once more on his cheeks. The weary muscles at the tops of his arms had taken flight. I grazed my calf in my attempts to fatten him up and gave David food every couple of hours. All sorts such as fruit, vegetables, meat, fish, nuts and anything with plenty of protein in. His weight continued to plummet so I telephoned the hospital. The nurse on call told me that any calorie was a good calorie as cancer gobbles up the calories, and to give him anything he desired. Not only was I baking homemade cakes but I started giving David what I call naughty food like doughnuts, sweets, chocolates etc. Anything he could eat. His taste buds were not working well and most of the time he did not want to eat as he could not taste the food properly, but he persevered. Nearly two stone was lost. I watched David's weight like a crow eyeing up a road kill. He had other problems like tingling in the balls of his feet which produced numbness. He bought some sheepskin ankle boots to keep his feet warm (very expensive!). Walking around the house in them David resembled a starved caveman searching for meat.

Backwards and forwards we went to the hospital for his chemotherapy and blood tests. David did not know what to wear in the wheelchair. With his weight loss, everything was hanging on him, but he also needed loose clothing around his legs what with the thrombosis, so I drove one morning up to Highfield Garden Centre where they sell clothes and bought David a James Pringle navy jogging bottom and matching sweatshirt. It was quite smart but casual. David would never normally wear joggers as he was quite dapper, but he was pleased that he did not have to go to the hospital in his pyjamas. It was the best I could do for him. I also gave him a colour coordinated blanket to go over his legs so he looked as smart as he could under such extenuating circumstances. I could see this made David a lot happier mentally.

The treatment continued week in, week out with short respites, but still we had to attend Dracula's Ward as even when he wasn't having chemotherapy he had to have blood tests and see the doctor. The next milestone was looming on the horizon. We were told that on the 23rd December we would have to attend the hospital for David to have his chemotherapy and then they would begin the treatment of thalidomide. They had postponed the thalidomide treatment for four weeks because of David's internal bleeding and clots in his leg. Thalidomide apparently can produce blood clots which obviously would be dangerous for David but he had to have the treatment, so they would be giving him a blood-thinning injection to counterbalance clotting. I began to feel shackled by panic and wondered whether they would get the treatment right. David would have to learn how to administer the daily injections himself a month before commencing with the thalidomide. I was concerned about David taking Thalidomide right on Christmas, but we were assured by the doctor that the hospital would still be working efficiently over Christmas if there was a problem. I could feel the winds of doubt gather pace and sweep across my mind. All I could visualise were drunks and drugged-up party-goers and all things vile. I shivered slightly at my preconception. The doctor continued to emphasise to me that if there were any problems or any bleeding from David via the mouth or his bowels to rush him immediately to the Accident and Emergency Department. Oh, the joys of Christmas! I would not be decking the halls with boughs of holly.

We arrived back home again. I went into my dining room. Richard and my granddaughter Jessie were originally arriving from Australia for Christmas but then Richard had to be called back for a week because of David's health crises, so the latter Christmas trip had to be cancelled. I had laid the Christmas table early and had shut the dining room off so I was prepared. I had to pack all my preparations away. I was so upset that my granddaughter was not coming at Christmas. I felt I had let her down as Jessie was so excited to visit us. She had shown me her suitcase on Skype she'd bought ready for the journey. I knew Jessie could not see her grandad in such an unfit state; it would have been terribly unfair and frightening for her. Anyway, David would not have been able to join in all the celebrations at Christmas as it was all he could do to rise ghostlike from his chair. Rick had made the emergency dash from Australia to David's bedside when he was in hospital. We could not make him travel again so soon. I had written all my Christmas cards early so I posted them well ahead of time and scrawled messages on envelopes informing everyone that David was very ill again. Some friends still supported me by telephoning. Alas one lifelong friend attacked me over the telephone because, although she was informed about David's problems, she felt she should have been the very first person to be told. She always had delusions of grandeur. I could not remember through all the traumas what person had been told first, and when, and found it very difficult to recite all David's ailments to everyone over the telephone as they were so complicated. Running headless, I was endeavouring to keep everyone briefed as best I could. Consequently, to keep the peace, I sent that friend a kindly letter explaining all David's complications and how hard it was for me to please everyone. It did not pacify her and subsequently our relationship has now terminated. I realised her reasoning had long since died. My emotions were ragged and torn. I had also forgotten my name and felt everyone else had. David told me I needed a punch bag in the corner of the lounge and should cut out the faces of all the people that had upset me and place them on the punch bag when appropriate.

We struggled through the days, David still losing weight. He had now resorted to going to bed with our Christmas box of biscuits which he devoured whenever he woke up in the night to go to the toilet. 2am, 3am, 4am, I could hear munching. That was just to keep his weight up. All I could do was pull the duvet over my head and hide like a tortoise in its shell. Then the light would go on at 8am, tablet time, and then off again. David was desperate to sleep with me as usual; and me with him, so we persevered. We had never slept in separate beds like most of our friends and we didn't want to be apart. We liked holding hands, mine warm, his cold. I begged for some more sleeping tablets from my doctor, but he had me on a strict regime. The doctor was worried I would become addicted. What did I care? Sleeping was much better than being awake.

*

Friday: Our weekly visit to the hospital for chemotherapy arrived. Just a quick visit or so, my husband told me. That was a joke. We arrived at the Edward Jenner Ward to find my husband's blood pressure was very low. They tested it when he lay down and when he stood up. It was dangerously low both times. The specialist had to be contacted and hubby was told to drink two litres of water, plus other drinks. I spent the following two hours wheeling him up and down to the toilet in his wheelchair. His blood pressure eventually started to climb, thank goodness. Then we were told he had to start the blood-thinning injections which took us by surprise as we were not ready for them. He was shown how to inject his stomach which he bravely did. I was asked if I wanted to try, but being a coward I declined. I knew in my heart I could do it if I had to. After hours at the hospital I drove us home. New roadworks had appeared at the top of the A38. Having been taken by surprise I tried to manoeuvre the car through them, but somehow I hit concrete blocks which scraped my wheel hubs. David bared his teeth and growled at me like a bear with a sore head as I had just had my car serviced and now I would probably have to have the tracking seen to again (which I did). We arrived back home for tea, six and a half hours after we had originally started off on our journey. I then had to throw hubby into the house as I had to rush to Tesco to get him some food. A never-ending miserable day, the likes of which I knew I had to get used to.

A new week began and we had to attend the hospital Thursday and Friday. I began to see little strides in the right direction. David was feeling a little better and I dropped him at the main entrance of the hospital without the wheelchair. He wanted to prove to himself, although very weak, that he could stagger to the Edward Jenner Ward, which he did. A blood test was taken followed by seeing the specialist. The specialist told us he could not believe how David was looking considering how wretched he looked a few weeks back when he visited him in the ward. That brought home the seriousness of his condition. Obviously the doctors had hidden their concern very well. The blood test came back normal except that his platelet levels were up. The highest they should have been was 300. David's were up to 518. Off the specialist went to speak to another doctor and returned to tell us that they had decided to do nothing about it for now as David was going to start the thalidomide along with the chemotherapy, and sometimes the thalidomide can bring down the platelet levels but they would be keeping a careful watch on them. David had by then got used to giving himself daily injections in his stomach. Our home had begun to resemble a chemist's. There were cupboards of tablets and a plastic container to put used needles in. He kept carrier bags of tablets he was not using regularly in big plastic bags in the dining room. David did not want to waste NHS (National Health Service) money but it was so difficult for him to explain to the nursing staff the tablets he needed and did not need, and the ones he still had at home. He methodically checked his well-planned out charts. If the tablets are actually passed to the patient the nurses cannot take the medication back to the pharmacy. David became very astute concerning the situation and eventually refused to take the tablets from the nurses until he was absolutely certain he needed them. The system can be very complicated and money wasting.

*

Friday: Travelled to the hospital. It was packed in Dracula's Ward and everyone was coughing and sniffing as it was the week before Christmas. The bugs were flying around the room and David was told to keep away from viruses as they were beginning the thalidomide treatment (this was a shock as we thought they were beginning the thalidomide treatment on Friday 23rd December), but there was no chance. They weighed him, checked his blood pressure and gave him a blood-thinning injection in his stomach, and started treatment. Back home we went through the snarling traffic, waiting to do the trip again on Friday 23rd December.

*

Saturday: The day began well. David seemed to have picked himself up from the floor and wanted to walk to the garage two doors down from us for the morning newspaper. That would be to him a milestone. Oh, the joy I felt because I didn't have to get dressed quickly to dash down there before the newspapers ran out. My daughter and grandson came around in the afternoon for a cup of tea. It was lovely as David played a football board game with our grandson which he hadn't done since he became ill with his second bout of cancer. I could see Jake's face light up as grampy, he felt, was getting better.

*

Monday: The day was chaotic as our gas boiler packed up. We had no heat or hot water. This was not good for David. I wrapped a blanket around him to keep him warm. We had to borrow a little electric heater from our daughter. I telephoned our gas boiler's emergency service. I was told by them that (even though I'd had the boiler serviced less than twelve months before) I would have to wait two to three weeks for an emergency service even though I had explained that my husband had cancer and he could not stay in the cold. The compassion from the woman on the end of the telephone was zero. Someone else's face to put on my punch bag! The world seemed crazy. My daughter's neighbour, thankfully, who was a registered plumber, rushed to our house and saved the day by doing a temporary job. We eventually needed a new boiler, which meant haemorrhaging more money!

The week after that went well except for a little hiccup when one night David's veins in his hands swelled up and he was in pain all night. We both immediately thought blood clots! When he eventually got washed and dressed in the morning David noticed the swelling had subsided and the pain was not quite so severe, thank goodness. Because we were told to keep a watchful eye on bleeding from mouth or back passage, or any signs of blood clotting we were both on tenderhooks. I even examined David's body for lumps. I had become paranoid running the race with death.

A jolly woman from social services saw me during the week to assess our situation. I was given a stack of paperwork to read through. It was a real mountain to climb and I felt I did not have the time to absorb everything. She had to eventually call on me again to go through all the details carefully. The woman informed me that the paperwork had increased significantly from the year before. I felt I was drowning in it. A carer needs weeks and weeks to organise the paperwork to get on the right track. It also takes months to get the wheels in motion. I told the woman from social services that David didn't need a wheelchair as we had one for emergencies and he didn't need any disability appliances as we could manage. Crossroads (support system for carers in the Gloucester area) also contacted me and I arranged with them for a cleaner to come every week for two hours to assist me. The cleaner could also keep an eye on David as she was first aid trained, which then enabled me, as usual, to take my ninety-year-old mother out for the day.

*

Friday: David and I travelled to the hospital for David to have his usual drips and injection in his stomach. It struck us how empty the Edward Jenner Ward was of patients; there was nobody in the waiting room! Were they all Christmas shopping? His treatment in the Chemotherapy Ward, which did have a few patients, took longer than usual. The wonderful nurses seemed more relaxed. I think they were in the Christmas spirit and I noticed patients had taken them in large tins of chocolates. I went for my usual coffee to find they had run out of their chocolate Christmas mallows. Very, very disappointing! By the time David had spoken to the specialist and had his treatment, we were the last ones in the ward. The night was stealthily creeping upon us, bringing with it Storm Barbara which made for a horrible, horrible trip home in the rain. We arrived at our destination and sighed a deep breath of relief.

We approached Christmas Day with optimism as we were going to my daughter's in the Cotswolds for Christmas dinner with her family. David, by then, thought he would be able to negotiate the steps up to her house. Pink carnations arrived in a basket from a dear friend Viv. Our spirits were picking themselves up from the ground. I felt it was safe enough by Christmas Eve night to take a sleeping tablet, yippee! David seemed to be on the up. How wrong could I be!

*

Christmas Day: I awoke in the morning – the bed was empty – and trundled downstairs to be greeted by David doubled up in the chair with his breathing very shallow. He told me he had been in agony all night and could not draw breath properly, but could not wake me. I felt awful that I had put myself first and thinking he was recovering well, had taken a sleeping tablet. I immediately telephoned the emergency number and the person on the other end said to get David straight to Cheltenham Hospital. I got dressed, stuffed all the Christmas presents in the back of the car (why, I didn't know), threw all David's medication into a bag with his pre-packed pyjamas and toiletries and drove to Cheltenham as fast as I could. As stated before, I do not know Cheltenham very well and was very nervous driving in a place I did not know. When I reached the hospital, after driving into three wrong car parks, I bundled David into the wheelchair and, with difficulty, shuffled with him to the entrance whereby I proceeded to race down desolate corridors and found my way to the Oncology Ward where they were waiting for us.

When we arrived at the ward I noticed two men in the beds who were seriously ill. Their wives, I spotted, were the same age as me. We all glanced at one another; one nodded to me. We all seemed resigned to our fates. David was in too much pain to get onto the bed he had been allocated and could not straighten up. The man across the room wired up to a drip was quite comatose and deathly grey. He lay with his mouth open, and with a deal of skill sipped at the stale fuggy air that choked the room. His wife stared blankly at the walls whilst looking patiently around the room, and tried to muster up a hint of interest in her surroundings. The other man I overheard had platelets which had stuck together. He could not swallow food, so the nursing staff, were relentlessly trying to sort the problem out. Eventually both men were admitted to other wards.

David by now was writhing in agony. I journeyed a few times to the desk nearby for help but the doctor refused to look up from his computer. I was invisible and he was deaf! Eventually I asked a nurse who was coughing, sniffing and flitting about like a moth around a lamp, with red tinsel teeny boppers bouncing on her head if she could help David, and could I have a word with her in the corridor. In the passage I described David's agony in the left side of his chest and about the unbearable pain that he informed me was spreading rapidly over his shoulder blade and down his arm. I told her I was concerned and queried if it was a heart attack. With determined hands grabbing at her hips and with her tongue like a two edged sword she spat out her bitter words and asked if I was attempting to undermine her profession? She stormed off, but it was remarkable that within two minutes they were doing an ECG (electrocardiogram) on David. David whispered to me it was a CYA. I asked him what he meant by that. He said it was because I had had a free and frank exchange of words in the corridor. If it had been a heart attack, there would have been trouble from me. CYA is Cover Your Ass! He was administered two doses of morphine by mouth which incredibly did not ease the agonizing pain. He could not lie flat on the bed, but eventually I got him sat up on it. A kindly woman arrived and, seeing the trauma going on in the ward, gave us each a Christmas dinner on a plastic tray. I sat there with the uneven tray on my lap, knowing it was impossible to eat my meal as my nerves had taken hold and had restricted my throat. She then popped back and gave me a bilious green Christmas cracker. Who was I going to pull it with? My husband was engulfed with pain. I stared down at the cheap cracker and it threw its eyes at me. It probably had a Christmas hat in it and a joke but I should not think a gift, not that I cared; the only gift I wanted was for David to be relieved of his pain. I don't know why but at that time of my life I felt like a sad character out of a Charles Dickens novel.

My daughter arrived after I telephoned her. It was really unfair for her to have to put up with all our disasters on Christmas Day. I was told by a doctor to go home as it would be hours before David could have his CT scan to see what the problem was. Not having any sense of direction and having forgotten the satellite navigation system, Zoe told me to follow her through the dank and dismal day to her home, which I obeyed. When we arrived she firmly told me not to get upset and cry in front of the children at Christmas. Having already taken in a deep breath and given myself a stern talking-to, I willed myself to sit on the happy step. After all, it was their special day and I respected that. I had some tea with them and asked about the presents they had received and let them open the gifts I had taken with me (I must have been psychic and knew I would be seeing them that day). We raced back to the hospital after getting a call from David. He had had his CT scan and apparently he had blood clots in his lungs, probably from the thalidomide. They continued to give him thalidomide to fight the cancer, but they decided to triple his blood-thinning injections in his stomach and had given him one of the injections at the hospital which allowed me to take him home. He was still in dreadful pain and found he could only take short shallow breaths which was quite frightening to watch. One amusing incident amongst all the misery was when the porter was wheeling David down the echoing corridors to have his CT scan. They turned a corner and there, stood as silently as falling snow, was Father Christmas in all his regalia. David thought he was hallucinating and took a photo of him with his iPad. He now tells us he knows where Father Christmas goes when he completes all of his rounds with his reindeers. He wanders up and down the deserted hospital corridors searching for poorly little children to bring joy to and brighten their day.

Zoe and I got David into the chariot again and I staggered with him into the freezing chains of darkness and glassy links of rain to Zoe's car. We eventually got to her home where I had abandoned my car. I was originally prepared to take David directly home but he had his bloody-minded head on and insisted he leant on us to get him slowly but surely up the steps to Zoe's house to see the grandchildren.

In tremendous pain and breathless, he got there and saw them. Gasping he put a yellow party hat on to lighten the atmosphere and Zoe and Jamie gave him his dinner they had saved and some of Rosie's (our granddaughter's) marvellous cheesecake she had made lovingly for everyone. I then had to get him home. Jamie our son-in-law held him under his arms, and with his legs giving way, we all manoeuvred him down the steps to the car and I drove home exhausted. How I longed to be pampered and pathetic like some useless women I knew -who cannot even drive – or cook, and are worshipped by their husbands, instead of having to be strong. Sometimes through no fault of his own I hated David because of all the fear and anxiety he was causing me, because my heart ached with so much love for him, if that makes any sense at all.

David's pain was so intense when we got home that I could not get him into bed, so David decided to sleep all night in his reclining chair with a blanket covering him. I put food and drink by his chair and placed his mobile phone on the arm and went to bed with my phone by my bedside. That was how we got through the night. I checked him a few times and, thankfully, he was sleeping peacefully which was a good sign. That is where he slept for four more nights. I was by then willing myself not to be ill; what would happen if I was? It was too sobering a thought. I did not want to get drunk on my doubts.

*

Boxing Day: The day had murmurings of hope in its brief light that smiled through the patio doors but I was stuck in my tomb as I could not desert David. I felt teary sat on the silent haunches of my bitterness, and felt the need to throw the recent pages of my life into a blazing fire. A helplessness, and sadness for David gnawed at my heart. I was grieving but he was still alive. We both at that time needed support although he was pretending to be strong for me. I knew, however, that I had to be the knight and wear the shining armour, but all I yearned for was someone to put their arms around me and fight the battles. I wanted to be seen again as a woman. How selfish was that? The tracks on my face were beginning to erupt with eczema which I had never suffered from in the past. I was ageing fast. Sometime in the future I knew I needed to get my hair styled and roots coloured. Thankfully, I had David's hair cut before Christmas.

All the BMW Motorbike Club members had a big meet at Whitminster on Boxing Day. I wanted to telephone someone and tell them to come and cheer us up but I did not want to spoil their day. I noticed a beautiful pheasant on the lawn gobbling up all the seeds that had fallen on the ground under the bird feeder. It was so therapeutic to watch. David and I, to our astonishment, spotted a Red Admiral butterfly on a shivering naked bush in the garden. Maybe it was a messenger from Heaven who had come to visit us and dust us with hope.

Bright butterflies of get well cards were still fluttering in for David. David telephoned his friend also called David who lived a few doors down from us. Dave arrived to sit with David to talk football which gave me time to have my roots coloured and my hair styled. Thank God for small mercies. I had telephoned in my hairdresser in the morning and got an appointment at 11am. I also telephoned the Calcot Spa and booked an appointment at 4.45pm to get my upper lip and brows waxed. I had to make use of the day. I arrived back from the beauty spa through icy roads and spewing heavy fog that had squatted on the on the top of the Cotswolds, and varnished my nails a shocking red in defiance. Thank God I had begun to feel human again.

David slept in his chair every night until we went to Gloucestershire Royal Hospital for our appointment on Thursday 29th December. We had to be in there at 9.30am. I had to scrape the icy breath of frost off the car with my bank card to take him. He was glued again to the wheelchair as he was short of breath because of the blood clots lingering in his lungs. We were seen by a chirpy specialist who informed us that David had to stop taking thalidomide immediately as it was too dangerous to continue because of the blood clots which had formed in his lungs after taking the drug for such a short period of time, but David had to continue with the high dosage injections in his stomach to stop the clots from getting any bigger. David discussed the pain in his chest with the doctor and we were told that there are no pain receptors in the lungs and the pain was originating from the diaphragm which was then sending signals to the nerves in other parts of the body such as the shoulder. I felt I was becoming quite experienced on medical matters listening to all the jargon. We were told that when he visited the Edward Jenner Ward for his following chemotherapy, the specialists would have decided whether they needed to administer another drug. David's face looked as haunted as a quiet moon and because his system had been so badly kicked about he did not want to take any new drugs. Alas, he was not a man to give up the ghost whatever the outcome.

We left the hospital and I drove David to the Gumstool Inn to have lunch. We telephoned our daughter and she arrived with her family to join us. We had a delicious lunch. I had endeavoured to get David out just for a short time into the real world. He needed normality. They were so caring at the Gumstool Inn, especially our lovely friendly barman James. They knew us well as we were regulars. The manager even ordered in San Miguel zero rating beer for David which he enjoyed as he could not drink alcohol with all the tablets he was on. By the time we finished our meal, I could see whey-faced David was not in a good place and slowly shrinking so

I drove him home quickly, leaving my daughter and family to finish their coffees and other drinks.

*

Monday: Took Mum to Bristol Eye Hospital to have a lens at the back of the eye operated on. She returned home but had to put eye drops in which caused quite a few problems as she insisted she could not put them in very well herself, but I told her she had to manage; after all, it was not rocket science. Later I heard that some elderly people (who knew my husband had cancer) had thought my brother and I should be going in every day at different times to administer them! I wonder if you become more selfish as you get older. Rapidly reaching seventy years of age, I wondered when I would have the honour of being old and to be number one.

I received a call the following day from the warden where my mother lives. My mother had taken all her tablets out of their blister packs and had put them in little pots and scattered them on her table which was very dangerous as she could not keep control of what tablets she was taking, and she would not use a dosette box. The warden was concerned as she is responsible for the elderly people's welfare, so passed the burden on to me. I knew if my mother collapsed that would be another disaster for me and my brother to deal with. All silly problems were building up and taking hold of me like an incurable disease.

On top of the melange of major health issues, minor concerns were beginning to grind me down. Silly things were going wrong in the home which I could not attend to. The sink in the bathroom was blocked. The garage door had dropped to one side and I could not put my car away. If I opened the garage door I could not shut it again and did not want David to have to struggle outside to see to it in the cold air. I had all the Christmas trimmings and tree to put away and could not get into the roof of the garage to collect the boxes they had to go in and was too afraid to climb the ladder. Like an itch you cannot scratch, things were beginning to irritate me. David had become snappy which was understandable, and I unfairly snapped back. I was so terribly tired and kept bursting into tears over nothing. Emotions were running riot. I was fed up with hearing on the telephone what a wonderful Christmas everyone had had as mine had been shit! My heart was hard and my soul was scorched.

I had decided to try and find a handyman that would do odd jobs for me but did not know where to look. David said despondently to me that I had a hope in Hell of finding anyone who would physically help me, even though I was going to pay them good money. Everyone nowadays prefers to sit behind a computer; it is an easier option. He was right, as always, because all the handymen were booked up as there are so few of them around now. Still, it was nearly night time again. Oh, the joy of crawling into bed to forget yet again another 'annus horribilis' day. One saving grace – yippee! – was that the doctor had again relented and given me some more Zopiclone sleeping tablets, 7.5mg, thank goodness.

*

Friday: David looked so much better, and whether it was starting on the steroids again or relief from the terrible pain which had subsided, he was straining on the leash like an overexcited dog to do something constructive. I polished and vacuumed the house and David retrieved his toolbox and went into the bathroom. I thought he was crazy, but my man of action sat quietly on a stool and repaired the bathroom sink. Oh, the joy of having a man who could do things. His smile spoke volumes as he told me he found working was far better than being alone with his thoughts. Maybe doing that one little job had, after all, been good therapy for him. Everyone was a winner.

David began to recover and his breathing slowly returned to normal and the pain each day was subsiding. He was happy to be back sleeping in our bed after those previous nights in the chair which was wonderful for both of us. I watched him out of the corner of my eye the first night in our bedroom, as he undressed. The light brown snaking was still on his leg from the clots. Although his muscles were still weak and his skin still hung loosely, he was beginning to gain weight. He had many purple circles on his stomach where he was inserting daily injections. Because David had changed his dosage, he was given slightly larger needles and this was the cause of the bruising. He was, however, quite pleased with the new, bigger, yellow plastic bucket they had given him from the hospital which he put his used needles in. My daughter said we should put tinsel around it and put in on the windowsill as a main feature in our house!

*

Another dull, miserable day began. David's car needed its MOT so we took it up to our nearby garage with David tightly wrapped up against the elements, and arrived back home. At teatime, in the unwashed sheet of the evening, I took him to pick the car up from the local garage. I had just departed from the house and stopped in the road as a bus was indicating and pulling out of the parking bay. Suddenly a car, whilst I was stationary, smashed into the back of my Citroen C1. I hopped out of my car to find it was a scruffy hoodie who was driving and wasn't looking where he was going. I immediately noticed a weather beaten parking fine still attached to his windscreen and instantly knew who I was dealing with. Words were exchanged between the three of us, tinged with threats, although everyone was trying to keep as calm as possible. The last thing I needed was David with cancer stood in the freezing breath of night arguing. We later found out the damage to my car would cost £300 to repair and I was only doing a good deed by taking David to the garage. I was beginning to lose faith and felt somebody in the universe really didn't like me!

*

Saturday: Another joyful day arrived. A copy of a letter arrived from the specialist at the hospital showing us what he had sent to our local doctor as he had asked for a report. I kept that letter as I always felt David had so many ailments that when I recited them to people they thought I was exaggerating and making up stories. I then had proof that what I had said was true. I had been thinking on that day of all the tablets, cream, injections and drips David had been on:

Chemotherapy (Bendamustine)

Thalidomide

Steroids (Dexamethasone)

Daily blood-thinning injections

Anti-viral tablets (Aciclovir)

Anti-mouth fungal tablets (Trimoxazole)

Thyroid tablets (Levothyroxine)

Anti-sickness tablets

Ranitadine

Aspirin
Codeine
Aqueous Emollient Cream for skin
Morphine Tablets (Zomorph)
Buscopan

*

Sunday: The day arrived loud and unruly. Its lamenting and cursing could be heard whipping across the fields. David picked up a cold. A shiver went through me. Nobody telephoned today. I had noticed the calls getting less and less. People were disappearing over the mantle of the earth. I didn't blame them; we must be so depressing. Woe lingered in a corner of our home.

*

Monday: I telephoned the doctor about David's flu like symptoms and she gave us an antibiotic prescription if things got worse, which was reassuring. We did not want to waste NHS (National Health Service) money and would only take the prescription to the chemist if needed. David telephoned the lad who pranged my car and he told us he had no money to pay for the damage. He told us to send our estimate to his insurer. I eventually took the car to the nearby garage and paid for the repairs myself as I could not go through the hassle and paperwork contacting the insurance companies.

I had a call from the University Student Support Team and was told I had passed my Tutor Marked Assessment 02 (my second examination) with 60 per cent. I was ecstatic. How the Hell did I do that? I do not know. They then stopped my course until October. It was heart-breaking when I put on my computer and found everything wiped off from the Open University. They have, however, kept my two pass results until I begin studying again. I had another lovely email from the Stroud Writers' Circle and knew I must endeavour to attend and get my life back to some semblance of normality.

*

Tuesday: My brother had to take my mother to the Bristol Eye Hospital to have a cataract removed (more problems with her eyes).

*

Thursday: Went to see a dietician at Cheltenham Hospital with David but she did not tell us anything we did not know. We had to go there as apparently we were told by our local doctor that they had had a dietician at our surgery but with cutbacks had not had one for years. I found this peculiar as there appears to be such an increase in obesity I felt it would be essential to have dieticians on hand locally for anyone who needed them. The odd information the dietician gave us was to use dried Marvel milk in any drinks or food David could put it in as it contains double the protein that ordinary milk contains. I hadn't seen it for years but, luckily, a Tesco supermarket assistant found some in the baking section. We then dashed from Cheltenham Hospital to Gloucestershire Royal Hospital to see a specialist. He was stunned at how David had recuperated due to the journey he had been on. Our daughter met us and listened in to the conversation. We chuckled to ourselves when we departed as David turned around to us and said how he would like to see a positive sign of how well he was recuperating. This was said as he was walking down the corridors of the hospital! My daughter burst out laughing and asked him what he thought he was doing at that moment in time after spending so much time being pushed around in his chariot of fire. What more proof did he need!

*

Friday: David went through the usual chemotherapy. Petrol was costing us a fortune. Later, after injecting himself in the stomach, David bled the rest of the day and through the night. I had to change our sheets the following morning as they were covered in blood even though David had put plasters on his stomach. I telephoned the emergency number of the hospital to let them know what had happened. Maybe his blood had turned to water? The staff told us he must have injected himself through a blood vessel and not to worry, but to let them know if the bleeding did not stop, which thankfully it did after compressing David's stomach for a while as instructed.

*

Sunday: David weighed himself and found he had put on another half a stone. His face was fiery red and sore and he had broken out in spots. We have to keep a watchful eye on his skin as it is dry and delicate because of his different ailments and medication. David has to continuously put cream on his face and parts of his body daily, mainly due to his haemachromatosis and now his chemotherapy treatment. Yet another prescription for life! He must never be exposed to the sun for very long periods, if at all. I have to keep him mostly in the shade or dark. I think I have married a bat. All he has to do now is hang upside down in his garage!

*

Tuesday: My brother took my mother to the doctors' as it was thought by her warden that she was showing signs of dementia. The warden thought Mum needed a memory test.

*

Wednesday: Sinking again, I read the carers' booklet which showed coffee mornings were being held on Wednesdays locally for carers to attend and have a chat and meet people in the same position as themselves. I willed myself to dress up, put my make-up on and go. I arrived and was told that the coffee morning had been cancelled. Although I did not know the circumstances why, I got home more fed up and suicidal than when l left. On top of that I had given up my Salsa classes as I was too concerned to leave David for too long on his own and knew I would feel a pang of guilt dancing away when David was not well, although he tried to encourage me to continue.

I finally completed the last of the Gloucestershire Carers' Group paperwork which was given to me. A woman called Jane eventually helped me fill in all the necessary documentation which I was eternally grateful for and now I am a Registered Carer. The emergency scheme is at last in place and I have the emergency number on the door of my refrigerator which gives reassurance.

*

Friday: We went back to hospital again for David's chemotherapy to be told by the specialist that this last bout of cancer had been very aggressive and had taken them by surprise. We were also told that there would be no cure; therefore, the best they would be able to do in the future would be to monitor him carefully which would mean a blood test once a month to check his protein levels. If there was a change in the reading, it would indicate the cancer had returned, and also a scan would have to be taken every three months. That was going to be our routine for the rest of David's life. It was the painful two words "no cure" that stuck in our craws. I was given a card which I have to keep on me at all times so that if David has an accident and needs a blood transfusion, the blood has to be radiated. We have a patient alert card because of the medication he is on for deep vein thrombosis. I also have to keep a card with David's number on me and an emergency telephone number, so if I contact the hospital they can look up his medical records immediately. We did have a giggle, however, when the specialist told us David's condition was so complicated he would hate his case study to be used in an examination for medical students!

*

Monday: Had to take Mum after her cataract operation to Specsavers to have new glasses. After many tests we got the prescription sorted out except for the hospital paperwork which mum had forgotten to take with her. They needed it urgently so I had to go back to her house and search. I was told that I had to take her back the following week for eye drops to be put in to enlarge her pupils to double check everything else was all right. Also, she had to attend Cossham Hospital for a brain scan because of her memory loss. She now forgets names, places and times but, thankfully, has not wandered down the road in her nightie or anything awful like that. I found what with mother's forgetfulness, and talking gobbledygook, and my husband talking nonsense because of all the drugs he is on, and his tiredness, I felt I was living in La La Land. All I wanted to do was to get back to my university course and find myself. My selfishness was creeping up on me again!

This was one of my weeks:
Monday: Took Mother to the mall for the day (usual routine)
Tuesday: Went to Specsavers for Mum's eye tests
Wednesday: Yippee! One day to myself. I managed to enter some short story and poetry competitions, so was working all day on my computer
Thursday: Took David to Gloucestershire Royal Hospital to see the specialist
Friday: Took David to hospital for his chemotherapy

On the Wednesday I had to myself, I sat and re-evaluated my life. I realised you are never so much alone as when you are in need. I would tell all carers to take any help that is offered to you. Do not be afraid to ask for assistance. Use the support groups that are out there. Do the best you can and do not feel guilty when you want some me time. You are very important.

I will now just hold on to the life raft with kindly people aboard and set adrift the ones that were not there in my hour of need. Life is about fighting for survival in the storm and tempest. I would like to thank my brother, some of my good friends, and some who were once just distant acquaintances but stood up to the mark and showed their true colours and stayed alongside David and I. I would like to thank them all from the bottom of my heart.

I would like to thank all the dedicated staff at the Edward Jenner Ward in the Gloucestershire Royal Hospital and the specialists for their kindness, also all the care support groups and cancer organisations who have supported us.

David and I would most importantly like to thank my darling daughter who always stood beside us; my son, bless him, who travelled across the world to help support us; our son-in-law; daughter-in-law and wonderful grandchildren who were there to brighten our days. They were our stars in the blackness of the night.

David and I feel at long last that we have resigned ourselves to the future. We both know we have a long and rugged path ahead of us as we know cancer will rear its ugly head again. David has taken care of me all my married life and it is now my turn to step up to the mark. I only hope I can do a wonderful job like he has done for me. I love him so much and will always be there for him, and pray that God will give me the strength to do just that.

They do say that God never gives you a cross that you cannot carry.

The gates of Hell have cracked open once again and my husband's cancer has reared its ugly head for a third time, ready to devour our world.